Printed in Great Britain
by Amazon

35109344R00067